HOW TO BE TEXAN

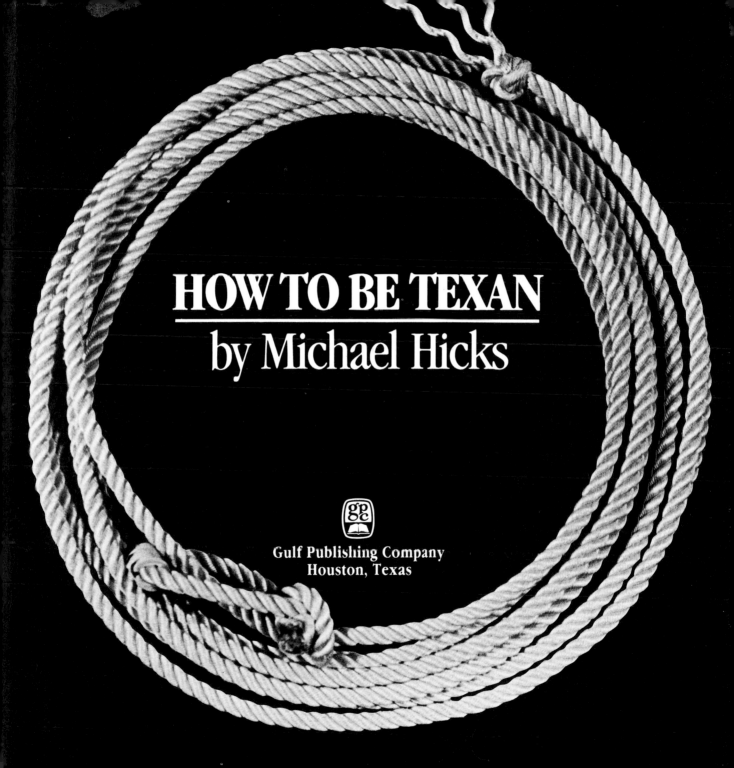

HOW TO BE TEXAN

by Michael Hicks

Gulf Publishing Company
Houston, Texas

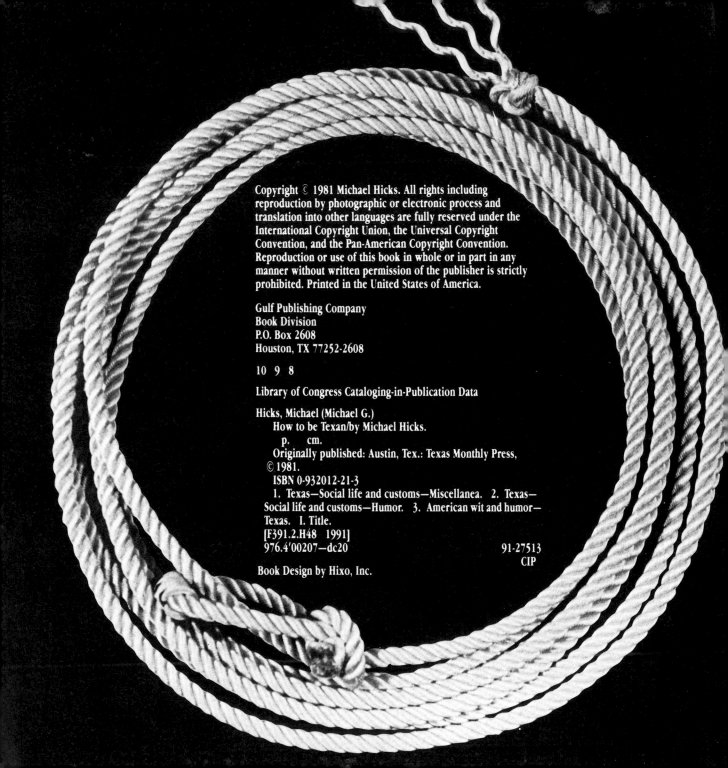

Gulf Publishing Company
Book Division
P.O. Box 2608
Houston, TX 77252-2608

10 9 8

Library of Congress Cataloging-in-Publication Data

Hicks, Michael (Michael G.)
    How to be Texan/by Michael Hicks.
        p.   cm.
    Originally published: Austin, Tex.: Texas Monthly Press,
©1981.
    ISBN 0-932012-21-3
    1. Texas—Social life and customs—Miscellanea. 2. Texas—
Social life and customs—Humor. 3. American wit and humor—
Texas. I. Title.
[F391.2.H48 1991]
976.4′00207—dc20   91-27513
                                              CIP

Book Design by Hixo, Inc.

Special thanks to Suzi Jean Sands for the original idea, Tommy Joe Poth for his complete knowledge of the state, and Dan Bob Okrent for his courage.

Illustrations by Mike Hicks, Patti Heid, Tom Curry, Tom Ballenger, Richard Krall, Tom Poth, Larry Jolly, Harrison Saunders, Carol Powell.

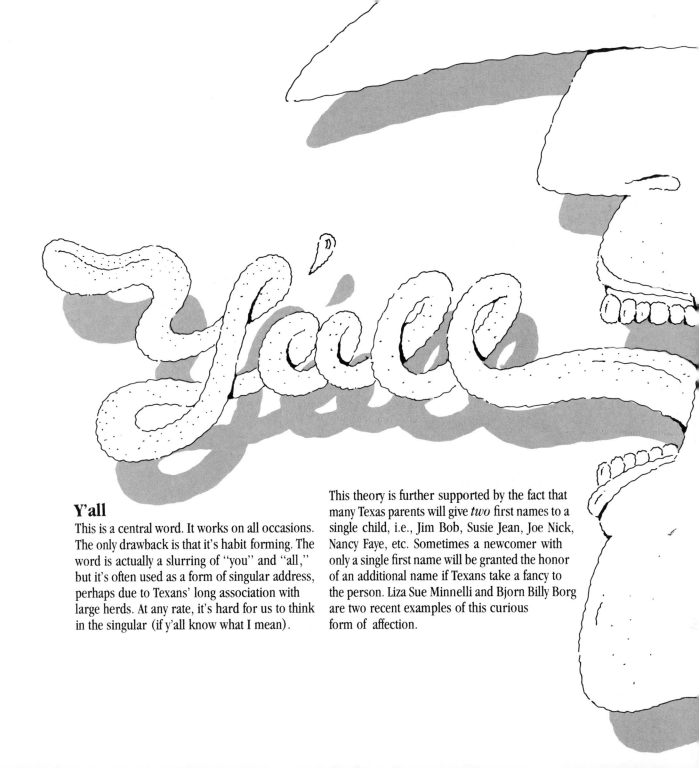

Y'all

This is a central word. It works on all occasions. The only drawback is that it's habit forming. The word is actually a slurring of "you" and "all," but it's often used as a form of singular address, perhaps due to Texans' long association with large herds. At any rate, it's hard for us to think in the singular (if y'all know what I mean).

This theory is further supported by the fact that many Texas parents will give *two* first names to a single child, i.e., Jim Bob, Susie Jean, Joe Nick, Nancy Faye, etc. Sometimes a newcomer with only a single first name will be granted the honor of an additional name if Texans take a fancy to the person. Liza Sue Minnelli and Bjorn Billy Borg are two recent examples of this curious form of affection.

HATS

Cowboy hats come in as many styles as there are owners. Many people call all of them Stetsons when, in fact, Stetson is a brand name only. Because there are more styles and creases than we can list here, we'll give a brief description of four distinct styles and leave it up to you and your hatter to work out the fine details.

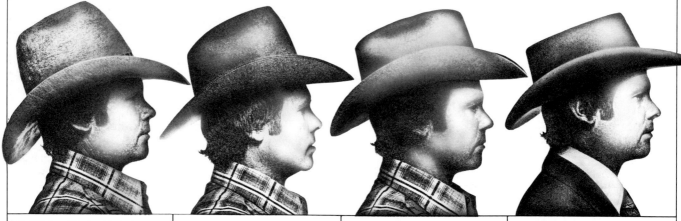

Bullrider—This hat changes with the seasons—straw in the summer, felt in the winter. It has a high crown that is slightly creased and the brim is pulled down in front and back but is wide on the sides. The name is a natural if you've ever seen a cowboy mount a bull in the chute, because just before he gets a good grip on the rope, he grabs his hat in back and front and pulls it on real good. Even if you start out with a fairly normal hat, several weeks of this treatment will transform it into a bullrider crease.

R.C.A.—This style is named for the Rodeo Cowboy Association. It has a high crown with side vents, a center crease that is wider at the back than the front, and a brim just wide enough to keep the sun out of your eyes. Comes in felt or straw, depending on the season.

Rancher—For the boss man and not the hired hand. Usually in beaver, this style has a wide brim and a high crown.

Hi-Roller—The descriptive name suits the wearer as well as the style. This is a favorite with the city cowboy and is preferred in either beaver or felt. It has a low crown with a rolled brim.

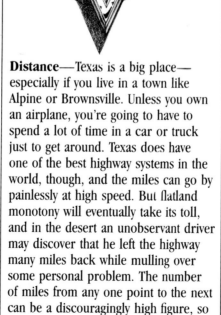

Native Texans have a primal attachment to automobiles. Only Californians come close to anything like the deep personal relationships that Texans develop with their cars and trucks. It's a holdover from the days of the horse. Texans think of the horse and the car as creatures with a common ancestry; they believe that each possesses a certain will of its own. This attitude partly explains some of the curious driving habits that you will encounter on the highways here.

Distance—Texas is a big place—especially if you live in a town like Alpine or Brownsville. Unless you own an airplane, you're going to have to spend a lot of time in a car or truck just to get around. Texas does have one of the best highway systems in the world, though, and the miles can go by painlessly at high speed. But flatland monotony will eventually take its toll, and in the desert an unobservant driver may discover that he left the highway many miles back while mulling over some personal problem. The number of miles from any one point to the next can be a discouragingly high figure, so some Texans log distance in terms of beers. Lubbock to Plainview, for instance, is about a three-beer drive. This

also has its limits. At a reasonable twenty miles per beer, trips of more than five hundred miles become tenuous at best and clearly impossible for anyone who weighs less than 130 pounds.

Youngsters—Texans, particularly Texans who live in the country, begin driving at an early age. Tractors and ranch trucks are often the learning machines, but children are generally weaned off ranchland and onto roads by their twelfth birthday. It's not uncommon for Texans to remember birthdays by the car that they were given at the time. Since most wind up driving the family car during some portion of their teens, car salesmen are always leery of family sedans at trade-in time. The suspension on cars gets just a little funky after crossing twenty or thirty miles of plowed cotton fields, and point-to-point racing (or "station wagon motocross") is a big attraction in West Texas.

Gasoline and Sex—Young Texans have a keen dislike of the OPEC nations, people who waste fuel oil to heat their homes, and anyone else responsible for increasing the price of gasoline, all because it ruins their sex lives. You see,

VEHICLES

Texas is full of pretty isolated places. What this means to a budding Joe Don Juan is that, as gasoline doubles in price, instead of having his choice of all the women in a two-hundred-mile radius, he may only be able to afford to cover a hundred-mile radius. Yankees might view this problem as ridiculous, but in many parts of Texas a hundred-mile radius (or 31,400 square miles) will yield fewer than fifteen women in any particular age group. In these circumstances the price of gas becomes the price of life. It's not a laughing matter.

Speed—Resentment of the 55 mph speed limit is almost universal in Texas. Even the Highway Patrol has little good to say about driving 55. If you're crossing New Jersey, the difference in traveling 55 mph and 70 mph doesn't matter much, but it adds four to five hours to a drive across Texas. And if you relate horses and autos, as we do here in Texas, it's obvious that 55 isn't anywhere close to a gallop in a car that has a top speed of 120 mph. It's more like a trot, and Texans don't like to think of themselves as only being allowed to trot.

Cadillacs—Texans love Cadillacs. Any shape and any size. The newer the better, but better an old Cadillac than a new anything else. It's not that you won't see other luxury cars in the state, it's just that this particular car is a Texas tradition. Even people who don't like Cadillacs will buy one or two as a sign of their success. There are also practical reasons for owning at least one, chief among them being the almost irrefutable fact that you can't break the law while driving a Cadillac. Political clout goes a long way in rural Texas, and nobody wants to bring big-time heat on themselves (especially in the form of a country justice of the peace) because of a minor traffic violation. As long as the rural powers-that-be drive Cadillacs, a certain immunity will be inherent in owning a car of the same make. The only shortcoming about Cadillacs is that you can't carry much besides people in them. Therefore, drivers who have stuff to haul are forced to spend at least some of their road time in pickups. It would seem an easy enough job for GM, knowing this, to produce the ultimate Texas vehicle: a 4x4 Seville pickup with a humpback camper and a steerhide interior.

Trucks, specifically pickups, are an integral part of life in Texas. The only pickups that are absolutely stock from the factory belong to corporations. The rest are fitted with various extras that can tell you much about the profession, tastes, and predilections of the owners. Pickups fall into one of two easily distinguishable categories: country or city. City trucks invariably have a fitted toolbox in the bed. Country trucks have the tools spread around liberally on the floor and dash of the cab for quick access. Rural drivers like to recall events in their lives by the dents in their trucks and will seldom go to the trouble of having one removed, regarding it as a sign of character. City pickup drivers consider a dent to be a defacement. City trucks have four-wheel drive (possibly for negotiating the treacherous parking garage ramps in the Galleria). Rural drivers view four-wheel drive as laughable (if you really get stuck, you'll need a tractor to get you out). City trucks are washed and have heavy-duty everything. Country trucks are much more organic and look as if gypsies and small animals live in them. City trucks have the look of Texas about them. Country trucks have Texas literally stuck all over them.

VEHICLES

City

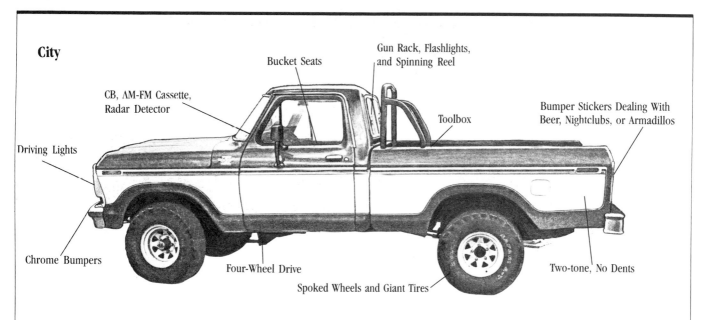

Bucket Seats

Gun Rack, Flashlights, and Spinning Reel

CB, AM-FM Cassette, Radar Detector

Toolbox

Bumper Stickers Dealing With Beer, Nightclubs, or Armadillos

Driving Lights

Chrome Bumpers

Four-Wheel Drive

Spoked Wheels and Giant Tires

Two-tone, No Dents

Country

Found-Objects Dash Containing Tobacco, Fencing Tools, Hot Sauce, Cigarette Lighters That Don't Work, Trash, Sticky Things, Bridles, Locks, Church Keys, Tab Tops, Receipts, CB Aerial, Beanbag Ashtray, Handle to the Driver's Window, Small Pieces of Wire, Old Checkbooks, Three Nickels, and Two Pennies

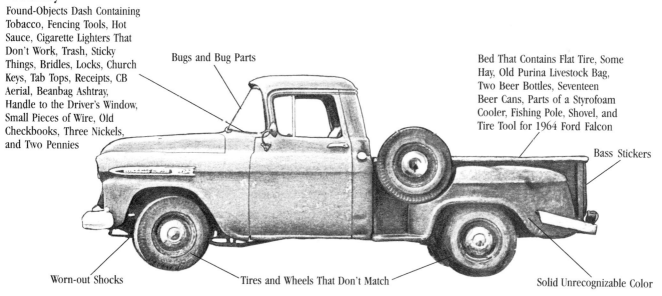

Bugs and Bug Parts

Bed That Contains Flat Tire, Some Hay, Old Purina Livestock Bag, Two Beer Bottles, Seventeen Beer Cans, Parts of a Styrofoam Cooler, Fishing Pole, Shovel, and Tire Tool for 1964 Ford Falcon

Bass Stickers

Worn-out Shocks

Tires and Wheels That Don't Match

Solid Unrecognizable Color

For a lot of Texans, steak is it. Period. Upon closer inspection, though, a traveler will find as wide a selection of taste choices in Texas as anywhere in the world. Texans do seem, however, to lean toward the extremely spicy or the extremely bland. Hot Chinese food from the Szechuan and Hunan provinces, for instance, is very popular in Texas. Of course, you can always get Italian, French, and other national foods in the big cities, but don't go looking for a spectacular fettuccine à la moo goo in Waco. You'll either be disappointed or arrested. As do most places, we have our specialties, and most are available in some form all over the state. Listed here are a few that should get you going.

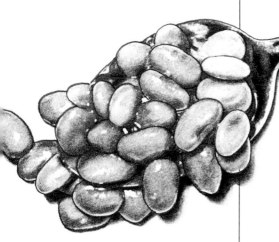

CHILI

This has got to be the official dish of the state. As you might imagine, there are several factions among Texas chili fanciers, the most notable being the "bean" and "no bean" proponents. Regardless of your affiliations, there seems to be a consensus that the hotter the mixture the better for the soul. There are chili parlors spread all over the state, and there are few restaurants that don't have some form of this local favorite on their menu. One note to travelers: some years ago, a retired anvil salesman is rumored to have requested kidney beans to be added to Wick Fowler's chili recipe; he has not been seen since. There is no such thing as a kidney bean in Texas. This is an inferior bean at best and the color alone should preclude its use in any dish served to humans. Pinto beans are the only suitable accompaniment for as noble a dish as Texas Red.

CHICKEN-FRIED STEAK

If anybody did a survey on the subject, it would probably show that most of the steak consumed by Texans is chicken-fried.

For those new to Texas, that's steak prepared in the style of fried chicken (as opposed to being fried by large chickens). Alas, finding a good chicken-fried steak in a major city can be a problem. It may be easy to find a bad one, but it will be tasteless and unchewable. A truly great one, on the other hand, is fork-tender, lightly breaded, crisply fried, and covered with Mom's good cream gravy. Although living in an urban environment seems to render most cooks powerless to produce an acceptable chicken-fried steak, this is one dish that you *will* be able to find in Waco. Remember, there is just one way to cook a chicken-fried steak; ordering it medium rare will only get you a round of hearty guffaws from everyone within hearing distance.

SAUSAGE

The humble sausage, more than any other food, reflects Texas' many ethnic influences. Some form of links are available in all areas of the state, and the more fortunate areas will have many different types to choose from. Of course, when all else fails, there's always Jimmy Dean. Some of our more notable specimens are listed below.

Chorizo—A mildly spicy ground pork sausage that is generally sold by the pound. The best chorizo is made by real chorizo lovers from pure pork and does *not* contain any menudo (cow's stomach), bacon rind, or ground-up day-old weenies. A gift from the Mexicans, good chorizo is delicious for breakfast when fried with huevos revueltos (scrambled eggs) and topped with picante sauce.

Boudin—Generally an import item from the swamplands of Cajun Louisiana that can be found in southern East Texas around the many enclaves of Louisiana expatriates. This link sausage has a fanatical following, many of whom will call their local boudin maker to reserve their week's supply. It is a fairly spicy sausage made with pork, parsley, chicken livers and gizzards, green onions, black pepper, rice, and a lot of loving care. Since boudin is pre-cooked, it can be, and often is, eaten cold as well as hot.

Bratwurst—A German immigrant and now a naturalized Texan found in areas of heavy German settlement. This mild link sausage, made of pork and veal seasoned with nutmeg, cinnamon, and black pepper, can be grilled, boiled, or broiled.

BBQ

You will find many different spellings for this in Texas, but the one most often used is simply "BBQ," or if you're dealing with an outstandingly lavish operation maybe "Bar-B-Q." This is another dish which Texans view and chew with reverence. A journey to an authentic Texas barbecue palace is as sacred a trip as a visit to a national shrine and a good deal more satisfying to many. True Texas BBQ is easily distinguished by the mesquite flavoring. Smoking BBQ with a mesquite wood fire over a 24-hour period will create a masterwork. Substituting pine will only result in a charred mess with no distinct flavor. Most other woods just won't cut it when it comes to good eating. Of course there are several schools of thought on this subject, so best do some product testing on your own. Don't worry if your BBQ is handed to you on a piece of butcher paper. This means it's the real thing. Also, don't worry too much about forks, and not at all unless you are served potato salad or beans. A restaurant that has a matched and unchipped table setting, complete with forks and water glasses, will probably serve terrible BBQ. It's a primitive food and should be eaten in a primitive style and setting to be enjoyed to its fullest.

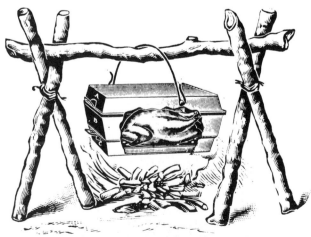

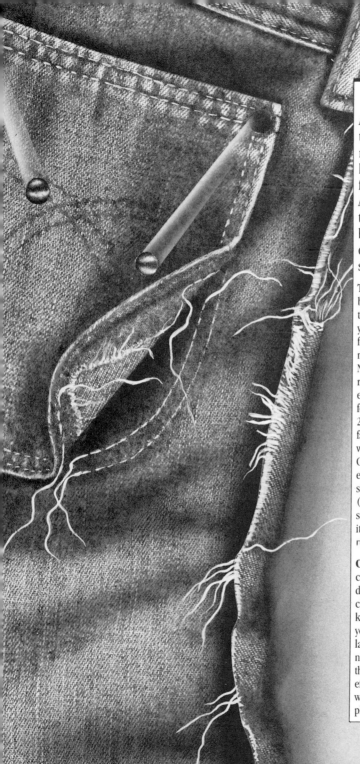

STYLE

A lot of what being Texan is about is style. The little things tell the story. For example, no flapping of the arms or gesturing is required for simple conversation. Not for cowboys, anyway. The key to all movement is contained energy. The only exceptions are funning and fighting; even then efficiency of motion is respected. And there's also the walk. It's kind of like riding a horse without the horse. You'll also notice a lack of jewelry, except for belt buckles and hatpins. Of course, you can get the little things down with practice. What you really need to know are the three sure signs of a buckaroo.

The Forty-Mile Squint—This is a biggie. First of all, close your eyes as tight as you can, pushing up with your cheeks and down with your forehead. Your hat should visibly move. Imagine acid in your eyes. Now, keeping all facial muscles taut, relax only your eyelids and open your eyes slightly. When properly performed, this exercise should create 275 separate wrinkles on your face—and everyone knows that wrinkles are a sign of character. Once you master the squint, use it each time you have to make a decision, pausing first for dramatic effect. (Note: Always try to direct your squints toward a horizon. Otherwise it may appear that you've spotted a roach on the wall.)

Outrider's Burn—Honest-to-Gawd cowpersons spend a lot of time outdoors, and most often they are clothed while out there. With this kind of knowledge at your fingertips, you can quickly figure out that flatland suntans will be limited to hands, neck, and the lower three quarters of the face. You can easily achieve this effect by applying sunscreen everywhere on your body except these places and lying by the pool for a

week. Once you've done this, you'll understand why there aren't many cowboys at the beach.

Jeanetics—Cowboys' jeans don't wear out in the normal places. The first signs of wear will be on the insides of the legs (from riding horses all day) and on the back pocket, where your tin of chewing tobacco is kept. A quick way to achieve this look with new jeans is to hire a person with fat legs to wear your jeans while jogging. He'll scrub the insides of the legs to pure white in only a few weeks. Sandpaper and a can of Skoal will give the back pocket the proper look. Cowgirls' jeans don't wear out at all; they explode. This is because cowgirls' jeans are worn skintight. The accepted procedure is to buy the jeans a full size too small, get them wet with a spray bottle so they'll stretch, pull them on, and then use a hair dryer to dry them. The jeans will shrink slightly while drying, for that reptilian fit Texans love so well. Dining with a cowgirl in tight jeans does have its hazards: four men recently received shrapnel-like rivet wounds when a cowgirl's appetite caused her Wranglers to explode in an Odessa restaurant.

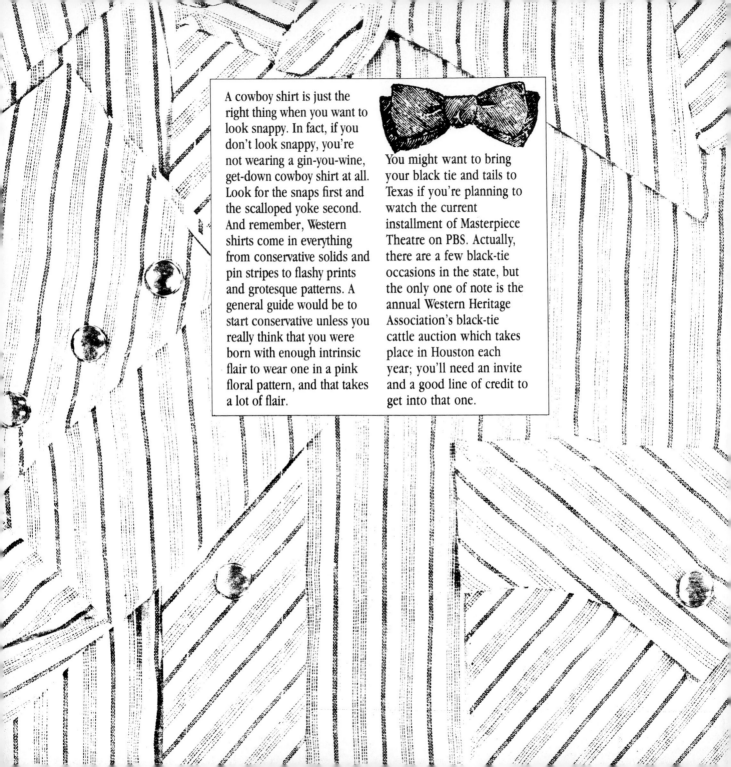

A cowboy shirt is just the right thing when you want to look snappy. In fact, if you don't look snappy, you're not wearing a gin-you-wine, get-down cowboy shirt at all. Look for the snaps first and the scalloped yoke second. And remember, Western shirts come in everything from conservative solids and pin stripes to flashy prints and grotesque patterns. A general guide would be to start conservative unless you really think that you were born with enough intrinsic flair to wear one in a pink floral pattern, and that takes a lot of flair.

You might want to bring your black tie and tails to Texas if you're planning to watch the current installment of Masterpiece Theatre on PBS. Actually, there are a few black-tie occasions in the state, but the only one of note is the annual Western Heritage Association's black-tie cattle auction which takes place in Houston each year; you'll need an invite and a good line of credit to get into that one.

RULES

1.

Don't mess with anyone on a Texas freeway. Some other places view a minor infraction of the traffic laws as a justification for yells or gestures, but here these casual gestures will be taken seriously. Remember, a lot of us are not used to big city life and as a consequence are already mad at the internal combustion machines and concrete. Add to this the fact that a lot of old West macho is still with us and you'll understand why jousting with automobiles is unfortunately becoming a common sight on some urban byways.

2.

Never call a *RŌ-dee-ō* a *rō-DAY-ō*. You shouldn't attend this particularly Texas form of entertainment unless you feel up to blending with the locals. If they think that you're slumming—and the latter pronunciation will give you away quicker than a snake can eat an egg—you'll find yourself ignored at best. Worse still, you'll miss a lot of the back porch viewpoints and insights that make small rodeos enjoyable in the first place.

THE KING RANCH

When you say "ranch" in Texas, many think first of the King Ranch. While there are still a number of large ranches left in the state, none epitomizes the heritage and traditions of Texas quite so well as the King Ranch. Established by Captain Richard King on July 25, 1853, it remains one of the largest ranches in the world. The more than 800,000 acres of the King Ranch are crossed by five hundred miles of roads and surrounded by two thousand miles of fences.

THE KING RANCH

This landmark operation has stayed intact largely by leading the ranching industry with innovations. Most notable among these was the creation of the now famous Santa Gertrudis breed of cattle, officially recognized in 1940 by the U.S. Department of Agriculture as the first distinctively American breed of beef cattle. Another King Ranch first was Wimpy, the first horse registered by the American Quarter Horse Association. These achievements are especially significant since both animals were the result of another, even more impressive King Ranch innovation: the Livestock Hatchery. Though cloaked in secrecy, the hatchery concept has been under constant development since the early forties by leaders in the veterinary sci-

ences. It took the King Ranch touch, however, to turn these visionaries' dreams into ranching reality. Even today, only a lucky few have been privy to the awesome spectacle of a Santa Gertrudis calf uttering that first cry as it emerges, full of life, from its shell. Naturally, the location of this giant hatchery and, in fact, its very existence, have been vehemently denied to the public.

The rumors persist, however, and a careful listener can occasionally overhear residents of Kleberg County speaking in hushed tones at local watering holes about the King eggs. Most remember the unfortunate rollover of a King Ranch egg transport truck on Highway 77 during the early sixties. Quick thinking on the part of a nearby Kingsville restaurateur created a beef omelet that fed the more than eighty people present at the cleanup site. Since this incident, the entire hatchery project has been clamped under tight security because of Texas ranchers' inherent distaste for "nesters" and the obvious impact that public knowledge of such a development would have on the breakfast food industry.

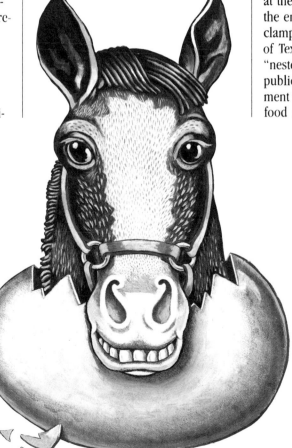

OTHER RANCHES

Having a ranch in Texas is much like owning expensive jewelry elsewhere. You just don't want everyone (read IRS, potential heirs, etc.) to know about it, especially if it's large. As a result, many extensive spreads are unidentified and unknown. A ranch's size can easily be determined, though, simply by counting the miles per gate (MPG). One MPG usually means a small ranch while twenty to thirty MPG lets you know you've got a big one. If you're not using MPG to describe the size of a ranch, then *please* use "sections." A section is one square mile of land, or 640 acres. Texas ranchers consider anything smaller than a section ridiculous. It's like giving your height in inches. Of course, there's more to a ranch than size. For the temporary Texan, what you raise can often be more interesting. For instance, there's *The Chicken Ranch* (La Grange). Perhaps the most widely known ranch in the U.S., especially considering that it's no longer an operating spread. Actually, the Chicken Ranch was a whorehouse of sorts, named in honor of the many thousands of chickens bartered for services. Tragically, the Chicken Ranch was brought to its knees and finally closed by a publicity-hungry newsman from Houston who was eager to get a five-minute news story. The legend lives on, though, in the successful stage musical *The Best Little Whorehouse in Texas*. Sadly, the authors overlooked the option of demanding their payment in chickens, and another Texas tradition bit the dust.

HOW TO STAY ALIVE IN TEXAS

Never tell a Texan his dog is too skinny.
Never drive in Houston after 2 p.m.
Never drive in Houston at all.
Always say "Howdy" to anyone who says
    "Howdy" to you.
Never get on a horse that someone says is
    "just a little frisky."
Never say anything about anybody unless asked.
Never cross a fence line unless it's yours.
Never eat anything that's "a little spicy."
Never wear a high roller hat or tuck
    your pants into your boots in a town
    of less than 50,000 population.

Never covet any woman whose husband's name
    is Billy Roy or Roy Del.
Never marry any girl in Uvalde unless her
    last name starts with a "B."
Never ask for the "soup du jour" in a town
    of less than 50,000 population.
The same goes for quiche, croissants, and crepes.
Never go deer hunting with business associates
    when a deal is being negotiated.
Never use the word "marvelous" in any
    establishment that serves liquor.
Never ask to see the tops of a stranger's boots.

One of the essential parts of any convincingly Texan outfit is the belt. And it can't be just any belt. It's got to be a genuine, made-in-Texas 100 per cent cowhide Western belt. Better to wear suspenders than to be seen anywhere in the state sporting one of those silly imitation cowboy belts with reflectors or Indian beads.

If you're pressed for time or forgot your *real* belt, then a plain tooled belt will do, but a real one will have your first or first and second names tooled on the back. If you have a first name that doesn't sound Western in any way, then simply add "Joe" or "Bob" to it. That way Texans will think maybe your grandfather was from the East before he came to his senses and moved to Texas. If you are shopping for a belt, remember two things: First, be dead sure that it's hand tooled. A Texan can recognize cheap machine tooling a block away. Second, you are supposed to select the buckle, loop, and tip separately. Beware of belts that already have buckles on them. There are two basic belt designs: the Ranger and the Western. It is largely a matter of personal preference which you choose. And don't be put off by the cost. You may find authentic Western belts a little expensive, but they are made from grade A, double-thick tooling leather and will often last for years and years, provided you exercise a little care and don't weigh over 350 pounds. If you weigh more than that, you should probably be using a tow chain and not a belt to hold your pants up anyway.

BUCKLES

Once you've selected your belt, then you have to find just the right buckle to set it off properly. This is a crucial step, so be sure you don't make a mistake. One of the biggest mistakes would be purchasing a plated buckle. That's because in Texas belt buckles are considered by many to be heirlooms passed down from father to son. Thus you don't want something that's going to get flaky in a few years. It's like getting a cheap watch from your grandfather. For this and many other reasons, you should buy a pure metal buckle, and that means silver. Silver is *the* precious metal in Texas. Gold is seldom seen except on the saddles of rodeo stars or on the fingers and wrists of millionaires. Almost all Texas jewelry is silver. Unfortunately, the popularity of Western wear has brought many low-life manufacturers into the market and made a simple thing like purchasing a silver buckle somewhat more complicated. Sterling silver used to be about the only silver around bucklemakers' shops, but now there are several other types. The most common alternatives are German silver (which is actually a nickel compound containing no

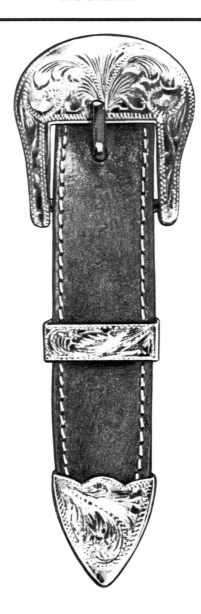

silver) and Mexican silver (which is 80 to 90 per cent silver mixed with copper and/or zinc). Both German and Mexican silver will last a lifetime and both can be engraved. However, each should be priced proportionately less than pure silver because of the lower silver content and the fact that the workmanship will likely not be as good. Mexican silver tends to have a slightly gold tone, which makes it suspect. Opt for sterling if at all possible. Do it for your kids. Do it for Texas. One last precaution: stay away from scenes, especially elaborate two-tone ones. There are some good ones, but they're few and far between. The traditional buckle designs have stood the test of time and should remain as attractive to your children's children as they are to you. If you choose carefully, your belt-and-buckle combination will give you pleasure for years, not to mention that it'll also hold up your pants. Creating a belt this way takes a little more time than just walking into Macy's and buying something off the shelf, but it's a personal statement. And that's what Texas traditions are all about in the first place.

GIMME CAPS

While a lot of cowboy hats are still worn in Texas, the most official day-to-day wear has to be the gimme cap. They are uniquely suited to the outdoors and, like T-shirts, eminently low-priced due to their advertising message. Hence, when you say "Gimme one of them caps," you get one. Of course, like all fashionable things, there are some that are more desirable than others. Seed dealers, farm equipment brands, and large cattle ranches are currently the most hubba-hubba logos to have on your hat since they all smack of authentic Texas connections. In fact, very few Texans would sink to the level of wearing any gimme cap that they had to pay for. They have more sense than that. If you are lucky enough to get a good brand cap, then please, learn how to fold it. Don't embarrass your benefactor or sponsor by wearing his hat in the style of an ingenue. If you have a John Deere cap on you should at least look like you would recognize a tractor if you saw one. Pictured is a correctly folded gimme cap. Three (count 'em) folds not only keep those great Texas sunsets out of your eyes but also allow you to stick the cap in your back pocket before you rinse your face in the water trough.

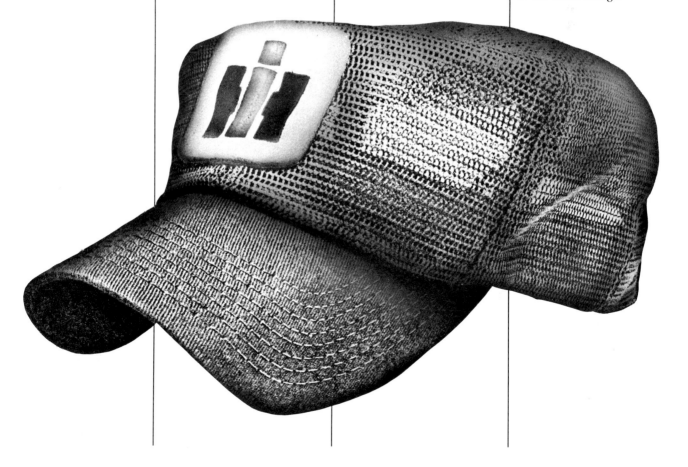

CRITTERS

Horned Toad—This spiky
little toad is a friend to all. For
sustenance it consumes
countless insects, which makes
it an ideal companion for
gardeners. Put two hundred
horned toads in your rutabaga
patch and you'll never have to
use insect foggers again.

Texas Prairie Chicken—
Currently an endangered
species. Not very good for
eating. They make a rather
unpleasant squawk.

Armadillo—These gentle,
stupid creatures live in the
Texas countryside but are being
driven farther and farther out
by encroaching housing
developments. Unfortunately,
the only place many urban
Texans ever see the armadillo
is flat on the highway. After
years of extensive on-site testing.
it is generally acknowledged
that the armadillo is neither
armored enough nor fast enough
to compete with the automobile.

CRITTERS

Coyote—This small predator has few friends in the Lone Star State. Though coyotes do take a certain number of chickens and other ranch animals, most claims of their viciousness are greatly exaggerated. Listening to their midnight singing and howling is definitely an acquired taste, but many people have been known to enjoy it.

Texas Longhorn—A lot of people think that Longhorns are quite plentiful in Texas, but due to centuries of cross-breeding there are actually very few pure specimens left. One of the largest herds in existence numbers only a few hundred and is maintained on the King Ranch in South Texas. If you have a powerful longing to see some of these noble creatures, you can go to Fort Griffin State Park, where another herd is kept.

Gulf Mosquito—Yet to be controlled by modern science, these brutes fly in from the swamps and backwaters of the Gulf during rainy seasons to infest some coastal Texas cities. While some reports cite calf-size varieties, most are actually no bigger than a man's fist.

TEXAS MYTHS

As one might imagine, in a state with as much wind as Texas, there's got to be a lot of hot air. There seems to be no end to the myths, legends, and just plain lies that emanate from the backlands and byways. Here are some that you will almost surely hear if you hang around for very long.

The Dead Skier

Every body of water in Texas large enough to float a boat will usually have three things in common with all other similar puddles around the state. It will be called a lake, people will water-ski on it, and there will be snakes (often water moccasins or cottonmouths) in it. On at least half of these "lakes" the same poor skier has been killed, apparently again and again. Here's how he died: "A friend of my cousin's was skiing out here back, oh, four or five years ago, down near the south end near the trees and they were seeing how close they could go to the logs . . . (YEAH) . . . well, one of his buddies tried to shoot between some stumps . . . (REALLY) . . . and they's all drunk so nobody was thinkin' about the cottonmouths . . . (OH, CHRIST) . . . and I tell you there's a lot of moccasins down there . . . well, anyway . . . this guy caught a tip on one of the stumps and fell . . . right into a nest of cottonmouths . . . (GAWD) . . . he was dead before he hit the water . . . when they finally got him out there's over a hundred snakebites on his body. . . ." When you hear this one, act real distant and solemn, appear to be fighting back some choking emotion, and quietly ask that your acquaintance not continue with the story, since that skier was your kid brother.

Hippie Hollow

There was a time when nude or topless swimmers frequented a spot on Lake Travis near Austin known as Hippie Hollow. But the fiction has grown larger than the fact ever was. Now bass boats cruise slowly by, full of slightly drunk fishermen expecting to be pulled from their boats and gang-raped by nubile, drug-crazed hippie women. At the same time, strange people dressed in trenchcoats and carrying binoculars look out of vans in the parking lot while respectable women lock their car doors before they drive past. Forget it. Hippie Hollow now exists only in the minds of the terminally depraved. The nubile women are housewives and the dream is over.

The Flaming Whorehouse

Here's another one that was always done by someone's brother's friend's buddy. Texas schoolboys historically have an almost instinctive sense of where the nearest whorehouse is and how to get there. They're not entirely to blame, since the free-love movement never really happened in Texas. Hence, groups of them will from time to time set out on a four-to-five-hundred-mile saga/binge toward the border for a bit of industrial-strength frivolity. There are a lot of schoolboys in Texas, and consequently the bigger border towns are usually packed with a few thousand kids bent on making a name for themselves as world-class funsters. That's the reason one in ten men who grew up in Texas will recall in admiration the time old Bubba burned the Golden Palace to the ground after one of the ladies was so worn out that she refused to accommodate him one more time. This tale is usually followed by a long story about being chased until dawn by the police, the *federales*, and half the people in Juárez or Laredo or wherever the storyteller happens to have been. What a bunch of swill! The grim reality is that anyone foolish enough to torch a brothel in those towns will have their arms and legs mailed home by the powers of darkness and will never, never be seen again. But it makes a good story.

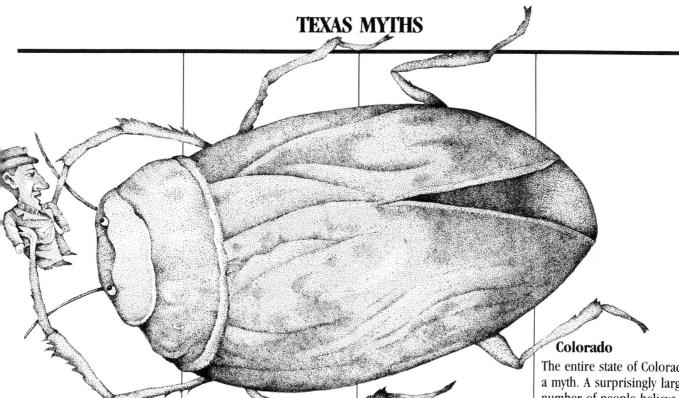

Houston Roaches

Due to a perfect combination of humidity, heat, and foliage, Houston became the roach-breeding capital of the world. This is no myth. What is a myth, however, are the sizes claimed by dismayed new-comers, many of whom have never previously dealt with anything so cunning and pre-historic as the Texas roach. Most people are repulsed by the roach simply on the basis of its appearance, without even considering that the roach is the only bug that will run away from you. It's this repulsion that is largely responsible for the exaggerated size. No one wants to admit being fright-ened by a little bitty bug, so everybody makes it a large, brutish insect. This keeps your macho intact. But enough is enough. Roaches in Houston seldom exceed four to five inches in length, and I person-ally have never seen one over six inches long inside a house.

The East Texas Bigfoot

Here's a creature with a healthy-sized stomping ground. Poor devil must spend all of his days running at top speed—or else he owns an old Chevy—to be seen in such distant places at almost the same time. Always late for those scary sightings. That's probably what makes the thing so mean. Reliable information strongly suggests that Bigfoot is in all likelihood just a de-ranged ex-4A high school foot-ball player in need of serious electrolysis.

Colorado

The entire state of Colorado is a myth. A surprisingly large number of people believe Col-orado to be a free, indepen-dent state and not just a resort area for Texans. The truth is that almost everyone who lives in Colorado is or was a Texan and some have been there so long that they've actually for-gotten. And so they don't un-derstand why there are so many Texans around every-where and they've begun to re-sent the fact that Texas sup-ports their economy. These misguided "Colorado citizens," as they call themselves, are to be pitied. Someday they will undoubtedly come to their senses and will live the rest of their lives in groveling shame.

BOOTS

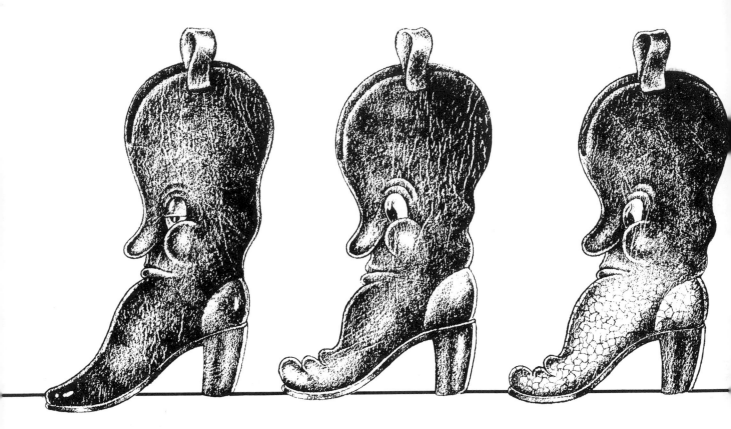

1. The proper way to wear boots in Texas. Buy your boots. Select something that is not absolutely covered with delicate leathers and western scenes. A straight brown leather, saddleheel pair will do nicely.

2. Take them home (or to your hotel) and find a rough-textured surface like a driveway. Now, beat and scrape your new boots until they're dented, bruised, and scarred deep enough to expose the lighter colored leather under the skin.

3. Fill your bathtub or sink and soak the boots in water up to about the ankles for an hour. Pour the water out and put them on. They will stretch and fit your feet exactly. Keeping your boots on, dry them quickly in a hot oven or with a hair dryer.

BOOTS

4. Find some mud or fresh manure (available at most better nurseries) and pack it all around your boots. Get the mud real wet so that it will get caked around the soles and in the stitching. Now, take your boots off and put them back in the oven at low heat until they are thoroughly dry (being sure to leave as much on them as possible).

5. Take a butter knife and scrape off as much of the mud as you can. Put your boots on and stomp around, shaking off most of the remaining dirt.

6. Your boots are now ready to wear. Be careful not to prop your feet up on any expensive upholstered furniture for a few days, until your boots have fully cured. There's nothing worse than some green horn walking into an official get-down country affair with new boots on. He'll be ridiculed without mercy.

MUSIC

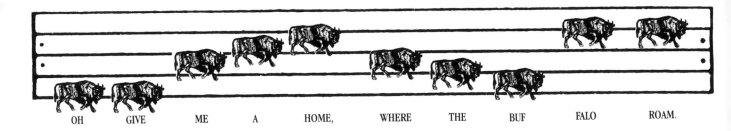

OH   GIVE   ME   A   HOME,   WHERE   THE   BUF   FALO   ROAM.

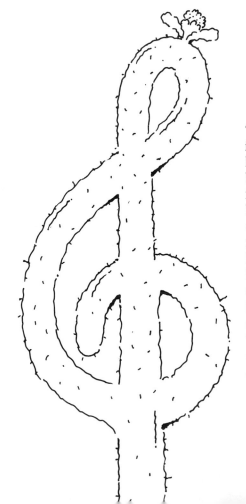

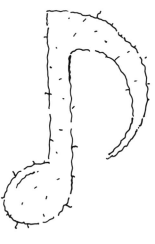

"Cowboy" or Western music has a lot of its roots in Texas. While the state is well-known for its thousands of Western bands, some of the best music comes from quarters very foreign to roaming buffalo and antelope. One unique form of music that Texas can lay claim to is zydeco, a blend of Texas blues and Louisiana Creole music named for snap beans. At a zydeco dance the snapping of the wrists is an imitation of snapping beans. In parish halls, supper clubs, and agricultural society buildings throughout Texas, you can hear forms of music seldom associated with the Lone Star State. *Conjunto* is a kind of Tex-Mex salsa played widely in Mexican communities, Bohemian-German brass groups play in many haunts in Central Texas, and there's always Texas blues.

RODEO

Rodeo is probably the sport most associated with Texas, and there are still a great number of rodeos which take place annually here. The oldest rodeo is the one in Pecos, which has been going on for 95 years now. The Houston Rodeo, which takes place simultaneously with the Houston Fat Stock Show, is probably the most glamorous, and the Southwestern Exposition, Fat Stock Show and Rodeo in Fort Worth may be the biggest and most official. However, there are an incredible number of smaller rodeos which are sponsored by townships, or fraternal clubs, or the FFA school groups. In West Texas, barrel racing is an accepted accomplishment for anyone's daughter. One of the rarely seen rodeo events is bull-pig, or boar bucking which can only be staged where there are a large supply of these monsters to ride. The sausage industry has, unfortunately, made this event almost obsolete in Texas rodeos today.

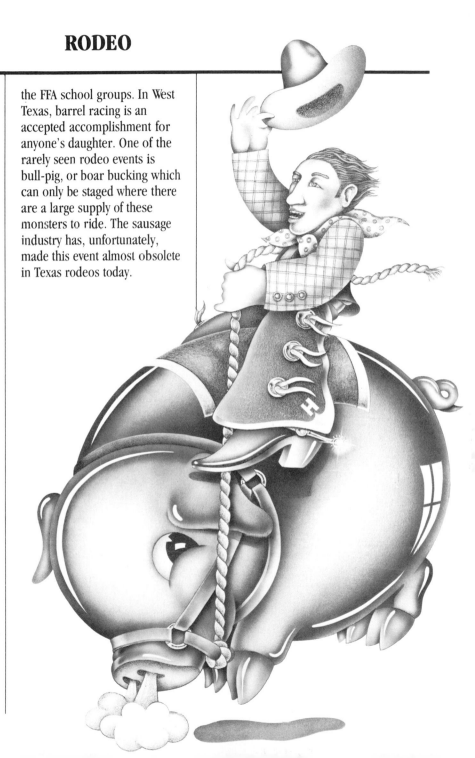

SHOPPING

Texas offers the visitor some unusual options for shopping. Don't be led astray into the millions of antique and crafts shops that lurk on every byway. They're as bad here as they are anywhere else. If you possess an insatiable curiosity about all such places, go to one of the flea markets on the weekend and get it out of your system. Then you'll be ready for the real stuff: sausage, saddles, souvenirs, and chicken feeders.

Saddle Shops—There are getting to be fewer and fewer of the good old kind, but those that are left are among the most interesting places in the state.

These shops offer some great buys, depending on your tastes. Among the most popular items are lariat bags, ropes, saddle blankets (call them rugs), mounted steer horns, and leather goods of all descriptions. One of the best saddle shops is Capitol Saddlery in Austin, run by Buck Steiner, who is a legend in his own right. Hint: Don't smart off to Buck or he might throw you out.

Smokehouses—Here's a way to enrich your life for days to come, as well as gain a few pounds in the process. Texas smokehouses make the best jerky in the world, probably

because jerky is the best thing in the world to eat while driving long distances, and this is a state with plenty of long distances. If you are suddenly caught in the throes of serious jerky lust, Central Texas is one of the few spots where you can satisfy it quickly. Of course, man cannot live by jerky alone (though at times it's tempting to try), and you'll find sausages, hams, bacons, and turkeys, as well as seasonal items. If you can't find what you want, then bring what you want (mother-in-law, pets, and so on) to the smokehouse folks and they'll smoke it for you. Many Texans consider establishing a good relationship

SHOPPING

with a country smokehouse a necessary part of their lifestyle. And for good reason: smoked meats last a long time, and most smokehouses will mail your orders to you even if you live out of state. It means that you don't have to accept the normal scrub that passes for breakfast meat in the average supermarket. You can instead get something real that has been smoked (not hickory-flavored), something that you know has been butchered and processed by honest-to-goodness human beings.

Souvenirs—Buying a real, get-down, bad-taste souvenir isn't unlike buying a pornographic magazine. You want to appear suddenly taken by it, spontaneous. You don't want people to think your house is full of this stuff. At the same time, you can't appear so hip that you insult the owner or operator who decided to stock it in the first place. It takes practice, but the rewards are great. Many places sell this stuff, but the righteous items require a search. The richest single source I have personally encountered is the KOA general store at San Luis Pass, which is a feast for the serious collector of ashtrays featuring aerial views of Dealey Plaza.

Farm and Ranch Supply—These stores are good for a host of things. Everybody needs at least one fencing tool. Galvanized tanks of all varieties make ideal outdoor planters or indoor coffee tables. A big ranch supply store will have clothing as well, and more often than not it's the kind that lasts long and costs little (you do have to get over the polyester stigma first). The trick to a successful shopping spree is in finding a reasonable use for what are obviously great things. Never forget, though, that not *everyone* thinks it's great to be served salad from a chicken feeder.

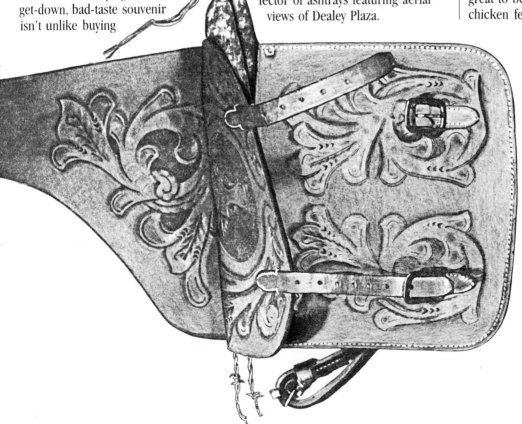

THE COAST

Texans seldom see much water in one place. And so, even though the waters off Texas beaches contain a good many additives and industrial by-products, we find a frolic in the muck quite enjoyable. Acting native requires but a scant knowledge of the particular locale. Even though folks new to the beach will be overcome by the spectacle of that much water and no fences, they can still increase their enjoyment immensely by remembering two crucial rules. First, don't sleep on the beach unless you are in an area that is fairly well protected from vehicle traffic. High-speed log smashing with 4x4 pickups is a popular nighttime sport, and when a driver is going 60 mph in the dark, sleeping bags bear a strong resemblance to logs. Second, wear some kind of shoes if you're strolling along an unknown beach. Chemicals and acids on the beach can put a nasty sunburn on the soles of your feet. Another consideration is that no one wants to hear you scream when your feet discover one of the 200 million jellyfish that have chosen Texas beaches to die on. Even if they have been dead for days, these brutes can still deliver a vicious sting to any fool who steps on their cleverly disguised tentacles.

Once you understand and observe the ground rules, you'll find an abundance of local Texas water sports and hobbies to enjoy. Some require a little practice, but almost any amateur can participate in these:

Shark Boxing—Now here's a challenging recreation. Texas coastal waters offer all types and sizes of sharks to

spar with. The silty, almost opaque water makes shark boxing a sport that tests hand-eye coordination as well as pure punching power. Only the great white shark will attack without first bumping a swimmer with its snout. Once you know this, it becomes child's play to cuff a shark on the nose when it approaches you and send it howling back into the deep water.

Hurricane Surfing—This one requires a little help from old Mother Nature, but few other sports can compare to the thrill of mounting your board and heading out to sea in a 150 mph gale. Besides, on the Gulf Coast, it's only during a hurricane that you'll be likely to see breakers higher than twelve inches. The fun begins with the first gale warnings and can continue for several days during a good blow. Experienced high-wind surfers book third-floor rooms in the Galvez Hotel as soon as the storm warnings are broadcast. When the big swells start coming in, you take the elevator to the second-floor lounge, have a few drinks, then catch a wave as it passes over the terrace observation deck. In a serious storm you'll be able to catch a wave right from your room's balcony.

Vacationers with a little time on their hands can also observe one of the most intriguing phenomena of the Texas coast: appliance collecting. Among many permanent beach residents, the stature of a man is judged by the number of discarded appliances that collect in his back yard. These totems of the industrial age are valued even if they're decayed, and some of the more complete collections reveal the entire history of refrigeration.

CULTURE

To understand Texas, you must first understand that there are no pure Texans in the true sense of the word. Texas has been occupied, settled, and occasionally deserted by an incredible number of different nationalities and ethnic groups. While some parts of the state were settled by immigrants from a single source (for instance, Czechoslovakians in La Grange, who have stayed put), most of the various groups have scattered. As a result, most of Texas is still under the influence of a two- or three-part mix of English, French, Spanish, Mexican, German, Italian or Cajun (which must be considered a nationality unto itself). Thus, in an area like Houston you will find French street names pronounced in a Spanish style, Spanish street names pronounced in French, and waterways referred to in Cajun terms. And this ethnic mix extends to most other areas of Texas life as well.

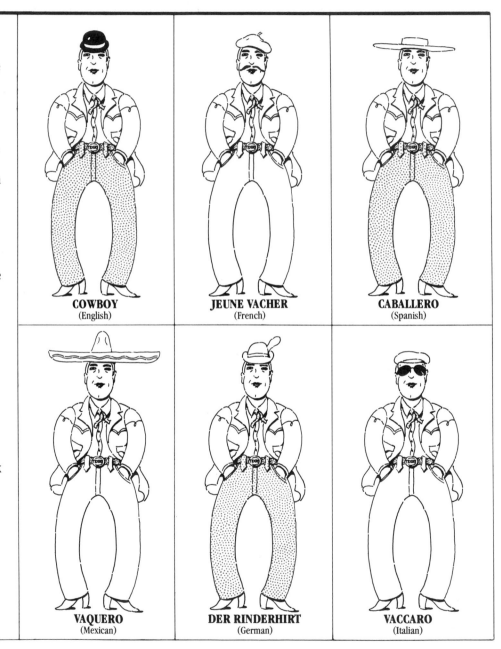

COWBOY
(English)

JEUNE VACHER
(French)

CABALLERO
(Spanish)

VAQUERO
(Mexican)

DER RINDERHIRT
(German)

VACCARO
(Italian)

DANCING

Texans are dancing fools. All across the state you'll find dance halls, clubs, and honky-tonks where Texans meet to trip the light fantastic or anything else that happens along. In dance halls you come to dance and drink a little. At clubs and honky-tonks you come to drink and dance a little. At either it's a good idea to locate the exits when you go in, in case you need to waltz out in a hurry. The best dance halls have several exits and a superior grade of sawdust; they usually cater to a diverse crowd, including families. If you leave one of these halls with dry clothing, you probably haven't had much fun. When you've had a good time, your clothes are sopping wet with a combination of sweat and beer, and your boots are covered in sawdust. Even a novice can see the necessity of wearing only pre-shrunk fashions to such an event. You'll see old hands wearing boots with Teflon soles, but this isn't recommended for amateur kickers. Don't expect to be able to get by in one of the good dance halls if all you know is the two-step. Some extremely advanced dancing takes place here. Here's a neat little step that will get you started at most places.

THE GRUENE SHUFFLE

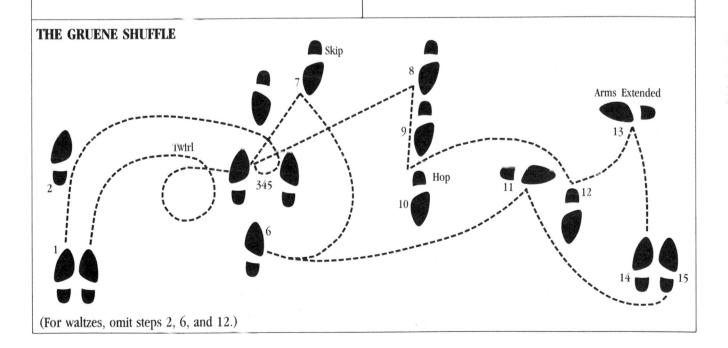

(For waltzes, omit steps 2, 6, and 12.)

PEPPERS

Peppers, particularly chile peppers, play an important part in Texas cuisine. Many foods here draw from the Mexican, Spanish, and American Indian cultures, and Texans frequently use chile peppers in some form to add spice and character to any number of dishes.

In much of the Southwest a dislike of chiles causes some degree of distrust, especially among any Texans present. Happily, though, you can develop a taste for chile peppers if you start slowly. Be forewarned, however, that it's easy to get burned while eating peppers. It's no fun having your tongue in a cast for a week, so here's a guide to the types of peppers you might encounter. It's always good to know what you're up against.

Note: Peppers, especially long ones, get hotter toward the stem. The seeds are very hot and can be discarded if you are preparing your own food. Avoid having need of a lip transplant by not letting any of the juice get on your lips, and don't rub your eyes if you've been handling hot peppers—unless you like pain.

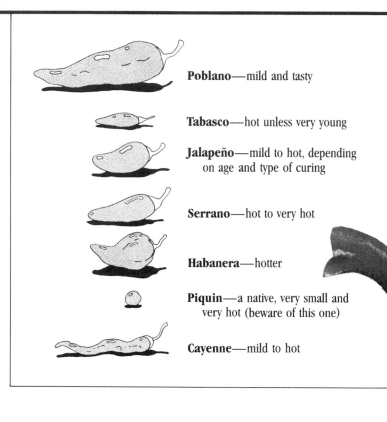

Poblano—mild and tasty

Tabasco—hot unless very young

Jalapeño—mild to hot, depending on age and type of curing

Serrano—hot to very hot

Habanera—hotter

Piquin—a native, very small and very hot (beware of this one)

Cayenne—mild to hot

MEXICAN FOOD

It's a widely acknowledged semi-truth that a great many Mexican restaurants use seven or eight key ingredients for almost every dish: beans, ground beef, chicken, pork, eggs, red or green sauce, onions and cheese. The trick is in deciding what order will yield the greatest amount of these ingredients. Is there more to be had in three soft beef tacos or two fajitas? Perhaps two chalupas will yield more of the same thing than a full order of special nachos. To get started in bulk thinking, refer to the handy tortilla chart below. Also be aware that there is an unethical fringe that will run odd-sized tortillas in on you, so pay attention to your neighbors' plates.

1. Large Burrito Tortilla (Flour Only)
2. Regular Burrito Tortilla (Flour or Corn), Rolled Baked Corn for Enchiladas
3. Taco Tortilla (Flour or Corn), Also Rolled and Fried for Flautas
4. Mini-Taco or Club Chalupa Chip (Corn Only)
5. Nacho Chip (Corn Only)

(Puffed pastries such as *empanadas* and sopaipillas are most often square-cut flour tortillas about the size of a taco.)

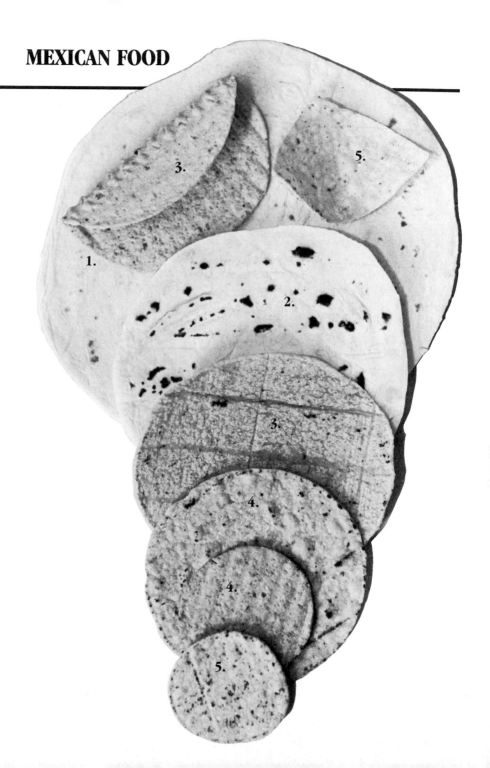

LUNCH IN A TORTILLA

Almost anything in the world—tuna fish, leftover macaroni and cheese, Spam—tastes better in a tortilla, with a little fresh salsa on it. This realization was responsible for the early experiments that ultimately led to the development of the modern fajita (*fa-HEE-ta*). Texans experimented independently in the early stages, but E. B. Poth was among the first to advance thinking in the field by placing the ingredients *inside* the tortilla. Prior to this essential step, pioneers had unsuccessfully attempted wrapping meat and salsa around the folded tortilla. The conventional thinking changed, and the practice of putting the filling inside spread rapidly. Soon a prototype of the fajita as we know it today was complete; the rest is history.

To put together your own fajita, you need but three ingredients: fresh flour tortillas, good flank steak (butterflied, salted, and grilled over a *very* hot fire), and fresh salsa. The fatty nature of flank steak makes it most unwise to use a gas barbecue grill (unless you don't mind burning all hair and clothing off your forearms). Once the meat is cooked, simply cut it into small pieces, place it in the tortilla, add salsa, and roll it all up. If you don't have *fresh* salsa, have something else for dinner. Without fresh salsa, it's impossible to have good fajitas. For your convenience, we have reproduced here the world's best salsa recipe:

6 jalapeño peppers, finely chopped
2 large tomatoes, chopped
2 large onions, chopped
1 small bunch of fresh cilantro, finely chopped
Juice of 1 lemon (or 2 limes)
3 cloves of garlic, finely chopped
3 tablespoons oil (olive, sesame, or corn—you choose)
Salt and pepper to taste

Mix all ingredients and let sit in refrigerator for a few hours. The salsa will last up to a week when refrigerated but will grow hotter each day. You can, of course, add more peppers or other vegetables, such as carrots, if you wish.

Frito Pie—This is the perfect Tex-Mex hybrid dish. It's made with chili, cheese, onions, and Frito corn chips, in a host of ways and with varying results. Although currently the baked version is served in Texas school system cafeterias, the original was made by taking a small package of Fritos, splitting it open at the top and pouring a ladle full of steaming hot chili inside. Fresh diced onions are then sprinkled on the chili and a layer of grated cheese is melted on top. The bag that holds the Fritos serves as a container for the whole mess, which can be eaten with fingers or a plastic fork. It's quick to prepare, very portable, and still served in this manner in some parts of the state.

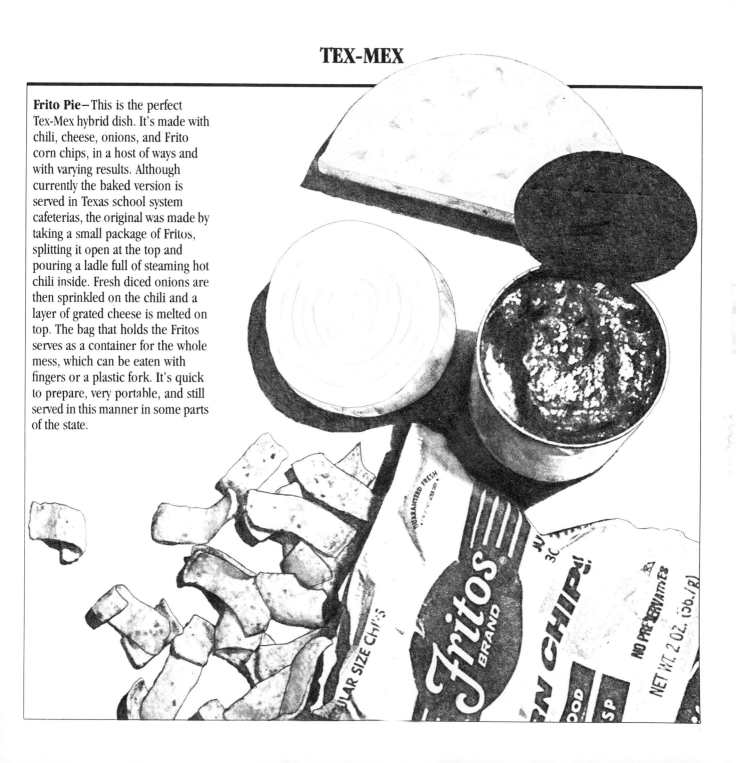

LIVESTOCK

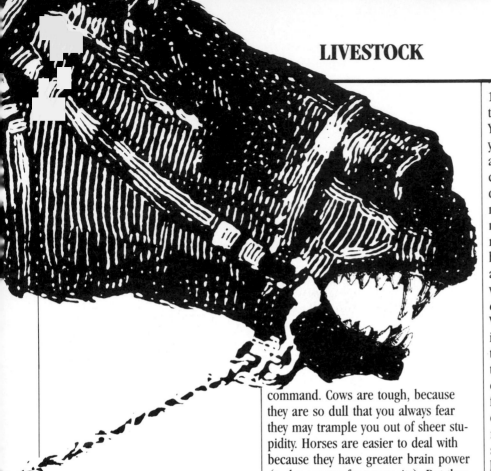

It's hard to hang around Texas too long without coming into contact with cows and horses. Unless you went to some fancy school or grew up on a farm that had livestock, it's unlikely that you've had very much experience with animals other than pets. No problem. Actually, a great number of native urban Texans are in the same position. They just can't admit it.

Understanding livestock takes an appreciation of an animal's fundamental stupidity and a willingness to kick, spur, or otherwise brutalize it into obeying your command. Cows are tough, because they are so dull that you always fear they may trample you out of sheer stupidity. Horses are easier to deal with because they have greater brain power (and a greater fear capacity). But they still will never do what you want them to, no matter how well trained they are. In fact, the better trained the animal, the more humiliating the experience. I personally have been embarrassed by almost every horse or cow I've ever met or attempted to ride and would have them all vaporized if I didn't like tradition and good steaks. But one man's trouble is another man's joy, and a lot of folks like to ride and rope and jump the great hulking dullards. Everyone gets forced into the situation a few times, so here are some pointers for survival:

1. Even if you're left-handed, don't try to get on the horse from the right side. Your dignity will suffer tremendously as you do a one-legged dance with the animal. **2**. Keep your machismo in a can and don't ride any animal that's described as "frisky but a pretty good mount." Take the oldest, most arthritic nag you can find. Even if the women are riding wild palominos (as they somehow often do), don't go for it. Insist on a horse over twenty years old. You won't be sorry. **3**. All of the above is *especially* true if you're dressed in new Western clothes. The best outfit to wear is a three-piece suit. **4**. If possible, be the last person to mount up. The worst thing in the world is to be barely in control of a horse at a standstill, waiting for others to saddle up. **5**. Watch the ears. A mad horse has flat ears. Either reason with the animal (pet or hit it) or say good-bye to your knees (horses have large teeth and rubber necks). **6**. You'll notice old riders at the stable or ranch giving you amused looks. Disregard them. They will come to New York City someday and you can get even then.

Oddly enough, many riders (even first-timers) find the undertaking pleasurable and relaxing. Ah, the wide-open spaces! Riding a well-trained animal on a sunny day can be an enjoyable experience. It's certainly one that Texans spend a lot of time and money on. If you become addicted to this pastime, the next thing you'll be needing is your own saddle.

SADDLES

If the average man's home is his castle, the cowboy's saddle is at least a semi-permanent residence. The saddle was the last item that cowpokes parted with when times were hard, and it was the cowboy's means to a living. The most notable feature of the Western saddle is its size. Designed for work, not play, these sturdy devils weigh between thirty and sixty pounds. There are three types of Western saddles: pleasure saddles, which are lightweight and comfortable; ornamental show saddles decorated with silver hardware and elaborately tooled leather; and roping saddles, which are wide and heavy with a low fork (see diagram) to maximize leverage against the rope. Most real cowpunching is done on a roping saddle.

Getting the proper fit in a saddle can be tough, since each manufacturer sizes them a little differently. Be sure to try it before you buy it, and don't accept a bad fit. You must also be certain that the saddle fits the horse. Under no circumstances should the saddle touch your horse's spine. The best way to ensure a proper fit for all parties is to take the horse to the saddle shop with you. (Well, nothing's easy.) Here's a saddle with the key parts labeled so you won't embarrass your horse at the saddle shop by not knowing what to call them:

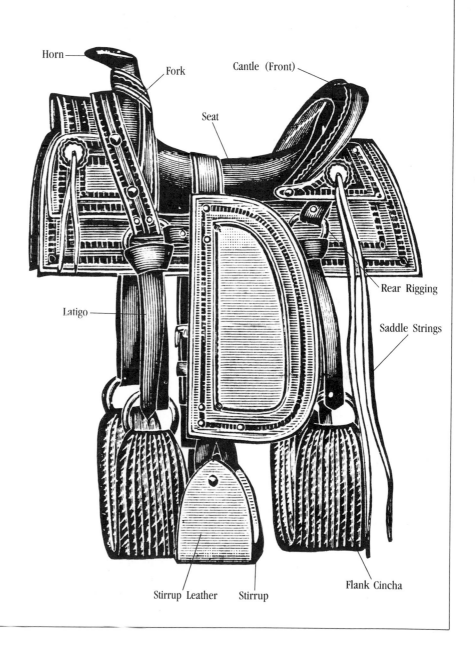

BARS

Every bar has established traditions and unspoken rules, whether it's in Spokane or Boston. The difference with Texas bars is that the chance that you'll be readily accepted with little ado is practically nil. Texans view their favorite bar as an extension of their home. Newcomers should recognize this subtle distinction and act accordingly. Here are a few pointers that should help you achieve acceptance:

1. Don't do a lot to attract attention, especially the violent kind. You will be observed closely, and ordering a complicated, "fun" drink or a glass of white wine will not go over well.

2. If you're intent on striking up a conversation with someone, start slow. Being a keen judge of facial expressions is helpful.

3. Avoid large groups and stay away from cowboys with no necks. Cowboys and ranch hands generally view other professions with disdain. Being an international banker is roughly on a par with owning a laundromat.

4. Avoid taking any kind of bet. Or be certain that you possess a complete knowledge of dominoes and card games, a black belt in the martial arts, and a fondness for tobacco.

5. If all of the above fail, claim to be an undercover agent for the FBI or profess having leprosy. Then they might leave you alone.

With careful planning, a few of the right exclamations at your disposal, and the proper appearance, you might not even have to worry about all of this. Here's the smart way: Check out the parking lot. A quick glance in the backs of trucks, an estimate of the ratio of pickups to cars, a count of horse trailers—all can tell you a lot about who's inside.

Take off your designer sport coat and try to look hot and tired (sweaty is even better). The first ten seconds after you enter are the most important. Look for the back door and then for where the regulars are gathered. Choose a place close but not adjoining the regulars. Sit at the bar if possible. Appear to be mulling over a personal tragedy. Don't ask for a list of beers, just say "Gimme a longneck." If you're determined to have something harder, then "Gimme a shot of your best/worst whiskey and a longneck" will do. Please, don't sip your whiskey. Glug it down in one violent swig and then take a four-second stare at the glass. In a resigned manner, put your shot glass down and take a long pull on your longneck. Next, a long, breathy "Whew" is in order. Then—and only then—look the place over casually but without any appreciable interest. From here on out, you're on your own.

THE LINGO

Texans talk funny. It's not for any reason other than that they choose to. They have a distinct dialect and they work at maintaining it. In fact, many are rather proud of it. If you believe it's a sign of ignorance, you're not going to be very happy here. The only other problem you might have is understanding what everyone's talking about. This can be remedied. It just requires listening very closely and watching for the reactions of people spoken to, as you would in any other foreign country. Here are some examples that will get you started on the right track:

SPOKEN	WRITTEN
Mayon	Man
Eggs-it	Exit
Ray-inch	Ranch
Day-ins	Dance
Bob war	Barbed wire
Thang cue	Thank you

One of the easiest ways of endearing yourself to Texans is to swear or exclaim imaginatively. A clever exclamation will include some poetic sense, a knowledge or familiarity of the country, and a little humor. The greatest exclamation in the last fifty years was spoken by a Brazoria County bull breeder upon seeing the Dallas Cowboys Cheerleaders' routine after having spent the previous three years of his life among the livestock. What he said was: "That beats anything I've ever helt, smelt, felt, slept with, or stepped in."

THE LAW

Law in Texas is much like law elsewhere, with some exceptions. For instance, in Texas, owning a pair of pliers or the Encyclopaedia Britannica would make you an outlaw, strictly speaking, since the former can cut fences (against the law) and the latter contains a formula for brewing liquor (ditto). Many such laws exist in Texas, since it's a lot easier to ignore them than it is to remove them from the books. Of course, some things can still get you in trouble quick:

Don't pick wildflowers growing by the highways—They don't belong to you. They don't even belong to Mother Nature. They belong to the Texas Highway Department. The Highway Department owns the land, it went to the trouble to plant the flowers, and it doesn't take kindly to anyone killing them. If you don't believe it, our highway patrolmen will explain it to you. Believe that.

Don't speed in Selma, Texas—The entire town is a radar trap. Even if you have a CB, a radar detector, State of Texas official license plates, and artificial legs, your chances of getting off with only a warning are still about four thousand to one.

Don't mess with a Texas Ranger—The Rangers are the oldest state law enforcement agency in the U.S. They still carry saddles in their cars and are not the best people to have mad at you. Founded to protect settlers while

Texas was at war with Mexico, the Rangers used a silver dollar with a star cut out of the center as their badge. Even today, this design is the basis for their badges. What few people realize, however, is that the early Ranger was expected to cut the star on his own badge using only his teeth. If you were tough enough to make your badge, you were tough enough to be a Ranger. Hence was born the expression "He just couldn't cut it," used to describe toothless small-town sheriffs.

AGGIES AND OTHER CLUBS

Graduates of Texas Agricultural and Mechanical College form the largest single club in Texas. They are considered the Polish of Texas. Aggies, as they are fondly called, appear in a great number of jokes that you will undoubtedly hear. In fact, it's hard to imagine being in Texas more than ten minutes without hearing at least one Aggie joke, so I will take this opportunity to tell you a couple.

> "Did you hear about the Aggie terrorist who was told to blow up the governor's car? He burned his lips on the exhaust pipe."

> "Did you hear why they had to put Astroturf on Kyle Field? To keep the homecoming queen from grazing during the halftime ceremonies."

Aggies get this kind of heat because they are an unusual group, set apart from mainstream college life. A&M began as a military school for men, and though today it's no longer necessary to be a Corps member or even a man, the traditions are strong. A&M is a first-rate school in several fields, however, and most Texans would still prefer an A&M veterinarian to all others. Probably because they're the best.

Texas has a great many other groups, clubs, and fraternities. Some are for the wealthy (Brook Hollow Golf Club has a $14,000 initiation fee), some are for the not-so-wealthy (Screwmen's Benevolent Association, open only to men who operate screw jacks), and some cover a broad range of the population (Texas Hereford Association, the oldest such group in the state).

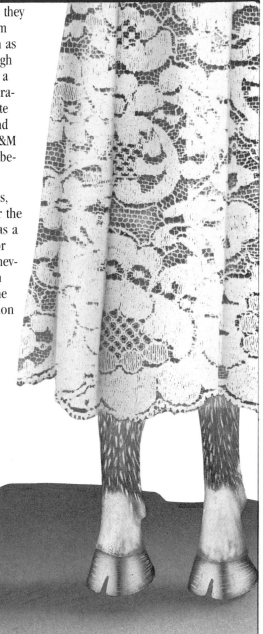

WEIRD PLACES

If the meek will inherit the earth, the proud will get Texas. Unlike the rest of the country, where people are obsessed with how old things are, Texans just like the things themselves. Throughout our state, one will find homage paid to mules, strawberries, boll weevils, etc. Also, many folks have spent a good deal of time and money preserving things that don't fall into the normal categories. Here are a few sights you shouldn't miss if you're in the neighborhood. Remember, with the right perspective, you'll find yourself enjoying things here that you might not notice elsewhere. They will at least broaden your mind to the human condition if they don't change your entire perspective on life and its follies.

Aquarena Springs, San Marcos

The springs and the surrounding amenities are but a backdrop for the real attraction: Ralph the Swimming Pig. Not only can Ralph swim; Ralph can dive. Few men, however worldly, traveled, and wise, can boast of having witnessed the wonder of a performing aquaswine. A must for the curious. Don't forget to pick up a few dozen postcards.

Port Arthur—Beaumont

Industry in action. At least once in your life you should actually *see*, *feel*, and *smell* what it takes to make your car go and your lights work.

Attwater Prairie Chicken Refuge, outside Eagle Lake

Thousands and thousands of these dull creatures come here to exchange gossip, meet new friends, and stay alive. Beware of entering into a conversation with any of the residents: prairie chickens are notorious for telling pointless jokes.

WEIRD PLACES

Enchanted Rock, north of Fredericksburg

The largest chunk of granite in the Southwest. A great place for imagining yourself as primitive man or for serious rock climbing. The place abounds with odd wind noises and other strange sounds. Even stranger are the people who come to hang-glide (rock-splatting, as it's called locally) on windy days.

Prairie Dog Town, Lubbock

Little in life's cornucopia can equal the almost childlike wonder many experience when listening to several thousand prairie dogs barking. So it seemed only natural to establish a protected colony of these rodents so that even people from out of state could witness this wonder. For centuries, these cute little fellows have been noted only for breaking the legs of horses and cattle with their burrow openings or for providing protein for hungry coyotes. Now you can make a quick dash (three to seven hours' drive from the major cities) to Lubbock and hear the colony yelp for hours. Lucky you, they never leave Lubbock.

Southwestern Exposition, Fat Stock Show, and Rodeo, Fort Worth

More of an event than a place, it nonetheless qualifies as unusual enough to be noted. A trip back in time to the old Texas and the many eccentricities of old Texans. Sort of a live tour of our heritage, good and bad. Unfortunately, it happens only once a year; look for it each spring.

Barton Springs, Austin

A large, natural spring-fed pool open all year long for swimmers, dippers, and floaters. The water temperature has been described as "bracing" by Arctic scuba divers and still represents the quickest method of achieving absolute sobriety for normal humans. The sporadic appearance of topless sunbathers attracts the leer jet set, and binoculars are not an uncommon sight on the west bank. Drop by if you're in the capital. There's always a good time to be had listening to the screams of newcomers as they hit the water.

TALKING CRUDE

If you want to invest in the oil business, all you have to do is mention it in any bar in downtown Houston and then wait for the calls. Everybody's got a deal. You'll be the last one in before word gets out, but you'll have to get the cash in the next two days. Sound familiar?

Texans grew up with oil. It was first discovered here in 1894, at Corsicana while the town was drilling for water. The workers struck oil at 1035 feet but persevered and finally got what they wanted at 2480 feet. At that time, oil was considered just a useless by-product of drilling for water. Things change.

If Texas were an independent nation (an attractive idea in oil circles), it would rank sixth in the world in oil and gas production. Consequently, it's hard to be here very long without hearing a lot of oil talk, which is almost a language unto itself. Here are some key terms that will help you understand the game.

My Hole Came In. Struck oil at a drilling site. Bingo! Cause for much celebration, back-slapping, drinking, and swearing.

Blowout. A gusher in the old days, a headache today. Oil under high pressure forces all the pipe and equipment out of the hole and shoots everywhere. A money-loser on land, blowouts can be very unfunny offshore, as a Texas governor recently found out. No one likes beaches that you stick to.

Core Samples. Cylindrical chunks of muck retrieved from drilling. By studying these, folks hope to find out whether a well in progress matches the logging reports. A match is supposed to mean there really is oil down there. Also used as a last-ditch effort to raise revenues to go deeper: "Look here at this last core sample! If we don't strike in another hundred feet I'll eat your sweatsocks. We're close!"

Wildcatter. Now called an "independent" due to the bad image created at banks by his predecessors. Fundamentally a gambler who plays with bigger chips and bones than most. These people have created a growing business in Houston for doctors specializing in ulcers and other stress-related disorders.

Roughnecks. The primary elements in drilling (aside from money). These itinerant laborers struggle to manage all the chaos and equipment associated with drilling. The work is hard and dirty, but the pay is great. The trick is growing old and still keeping all your arms and legs.

THE VALLEY

The Valley is a mystery. No one knows exactly what goes on down there. No one even knows exactly where it begins or ends. The term refers to the valley of the Rio Grande, but most people really mean anything in Texas south of the King Ranch. Most life in the area centers around Harlingen and McAllen. Known for citrus fruit, hurricanes, great beaches, and drug runners, the Valley might as well be a separate nation. Not many Texans have been there. It just doesn't seem right. Who ever heard of a lime ranch?

Another force in the Valley is the Aliens. Not just one kind, either. First there are the Legal Aliens, strange people from another land. Calling themselves snowbirds and living in mobile craft, they linger everywhere with no visible means of support. Local residents, though suspicious, have thus far accepted these strangers on the strength of their currency and their law-abiding nature. There's more than one kind of Alien in the Valley, however. The second (and more wily) variety is the Illegal Alien. According to citrus growers he doesn't exist, but people know better. There have been many sightings, but no one wants to talk about them. As harvest season approaches, their star cruisers and other craft can be seen riding low around back-street dining establishments. Witnesses are hard to find, but an artist's rendering of one of these creatures as described by observers is included below.

GROWING UP

Being a native Texan can mean a variety of things. The state is large enough and diverse enough that there's little chance that native Texans share a common background. People who have grown up in West Texas may have seen tornadoes, dust storms, and all the flatland in the world, but few have seen the ocean or more than three trees in the same place; Houston children, on the other hand, know how to surf and what to do with a tennis court. But one of the few things that any two people in the state might have in common is membership in the Future Farmers of America, the country club of Texas.

The FFA wasn't founded here, but Texas has the most chapters and the largest membership. Having been a member is a stronger bond than most would imagine, and few people ever throw their blue jackets away. Let's face it. If you were on the 1964 Dumas chapter Milk Judging Team and made it halfway to finals, you and your teammates downed a hundred or two gallons of bad, warm milk. That's a bond. It's hard to be a member without always finding yourself touching animals, usually in bad spots. Only members can buy FFA jackets, which may in part explain why they command a certain amount of respect. There aren't any pretenders out there wearing one. You want a jacket, you got to stick your hands in the back of this here turkey.

AUCTIONS

Texans are horse traders, and auctions are the chosen means. Most of us have attended auctions of one form or another, but the epitome of auctions and auctioneering in Texas is the livestock auction. If you don't mind the smell, you can see a great deal of country pomp and circumstance at a good livestock auction.

The only way to arrive at an auction is in a big pickup with a gooseneck trailer. Such equipment implies that you are more than a casual observer, and so you will receive some extra attention. First impressions are important, so don't blow it by showing up at a country auction in a foreign-made truck. These vehicles are good for nothing except trailering chickens and turkeys and are held in somewhat less than high esteem by cowpeople.

Auctions frequently occur in conjunction with other events—livestock shows, fairs, and the like—which provide interesting diversion for the casual auctiongoer. Most auctions also have good food and lots of beer. "A happy bidder bids more" is the idea, and it's

supported by much experience. There's the ever-present danger of becoming the owner of a large herd of cattle if you get too happy, though, so go easy the first time around. Fairly primitive methods suffice in settling debts after auc-

tions; most folks would rather part with their car than learn the fine points of stable cleaning over a period of a few years. Charge cards have a limited appeal to people who have always been opposed to plastic.

MILLIONAIRES

What can be said to offset the excesses of a tasteless few thousand Texas millionaires? Well, only that they represent a very, very small percentage of the group, and that all the others are well-mannered, self-effacing sorts with extremely good taste. The vulgar few have made the rest reluctant to admit to being millionaires. It's a shame, but with the good must come the bad.

Actually, a large group of people are affected by this stigma. It is widely believed that new residents of Texas often become millionaires within two years, but the grim truth is that the majority of newcomers have to wait far longer than that. Even today, with the countless opportunities in Texas, it's not unusual for a family to take up to six years to reach millionaire status.

It's quite easy to identify new millionaires. Not having been millionaires for long, they tend to buy ostentatious automobiles and houses, and they always talk about the money they've made. This is a far cry from the traditional Texas millionaires, who wear khaki pants and soiled white Western shirts and smoke cheap cigars. They can be spotted in courthouses trading tales with each other about how much money they've lost and what a hard time they're having. In spite of this, it's a wise precaution never to bend over in front of a Texas millionaire, especially if you're carrying a deed to anything.

HOLIDAYS

Texans love to party with other Texans, thousands of them whenever possible. That's why hundreds and hundreds of festivals and holidays are held throughout the backwaters and byways of our state. Picking the proper event is obviously important, since not everyone enjoys a full day of tossing cow chips in 90° weather. With the right event and the right perspective, however, you may have a good time doing something that other folks find disgusting. Texans know this to be true. These gatherings offer so many events that space would not allow even a partial listing of them here. Suffice it to say that there's little in life that is not celebrated at one time or another in our fair state; if you enjoy doing something twisted, just consult your calendar or state information agencies to find out who celebrates it. A few of the more standard diversions:

Snake Killing—This is a biggie. Everyone likes to kill a snake, especially a poisonous one. It makes the world a little safer. Spring brings with it rattlesnake roundups and chew-offs, so visitors should not forget to bring their double-thick boots, clubs, loopsticks, and other paraphernalia. Texans not only like killing snakes but get excited enough about it to try eating the things. So be prepared for Rattler Rockefeller and other strange derivations. Texas' largest rattlesnake roundup is held annually at Sweetwater.

Fests—Germans, Czechs, and Poles all like a good siege, and in the autumn all of them stage one festival or another. Beer, sausage, and a good time for all is the standard format. Bear in mind that we're talking about super-sized, heavy-duty cavorting, so plan on something big. Attending a superfest like the one in New Braunfels requires training, stamina, and the ability to find your way back to the hotel room while crawling. Newcomers should probably start with some of the smaller fests to get their feet wet.

DRIVE-INS

In Texas the only drive-ins of any consequence are for eating or socializing. This includes both the burger stand and the drive-in movie. In some places there have been enough other competing diversions to keep drive-ins from evolving to their full potential. But not in Texas. Here, drive-ins have developed almost to perfection, becoming state-of-the-art blends of entertainment, sanctuary, and social ritual.

Burger Stands—Don't waste your time with anything that calls itself a "restaurant" or that has the aura of a franchise. Very good burger stands may have several locations, but usually all are in the same town. One primary rule: you must be able to order, be served, and eat without ever leaving your car. With rare exceptions, the uglier the carhops, the better the food. If you're looking for good food (e.g., ranchburgers, steak fingers, corn dogs), it's best to go about one o'clock in the afternoon. By this time the kitchen has served anything that was left over from the night before and has had the entire lunch rush to get its act together. Don't be afraid to try local specialties; one of the handiest sources of the true culture of a particular town is its drive-in food. Of course, don't go overboard and order crawfish enchiladas without reserving a burger as a backup. And avoid secret sauces as you would the plague. Just because the carhop will eat it is no reason you should.

Movies—A really great drive-in movie takes the essentials of the burger stand and adds twin screens and a playground for the kiddies. Drive-in movies evolved in Texas to something beyond what they are in most other places. One special

Back Rows: Criminals, heavy drinkers, druggers, and people who can't make up their minds which feature to watch (so they park backward and watch one movie while listening to the other).

Rows 21–25: Serious heavy daters. Frosted-window area. Usually stop at rows 10–15 on the way out to find out what the movie was about.

Rows 16–20: Couples who are just starting to date or who have been married for more than five years. Double daters.

DRIVE-INS

characteristic of better Texas drive-ins is the elaborately painted scenes that decorate the backs of the screens. These giant murals are often the first encounter many folks have with "real ort" and account for more than one Texan's soft spot for neon.

Another variation on drive-in movies is the outdoor theater. It's just like an ordinary drive-in except that the cars are left outside. (Honest.) You simply haul all your junk through the gate with you. It's much like going to an outdoor rock concert. Be sure to take a few gallons of insect repellent; the mosquitoes in adjoining counties love to go to the movies. Unfortunately, outdoor theaters have by and large fallen on hard times, since any enterprising fellow with a big-screen TV and a barbecue grill can offer serious competition. Many of the regular drive-ins are still flourishing though, representing the last real cheap option for a family in chronic need of a baby-sitter. You just back the pickup into the parking slot, unfold the lawn chairs in the bed, and open your grocery bags of popcorn and your cooler of beer. If you doubt the popularity of drive-ins, check one out on $2-a-carload night when a Walt Disney feature is showing.

Novices should observe a few courtesies, such as not parking right beside someone else unless you have to and leaving your lights off as you exit (at least until you hit the gate). Don't eat drive-in pizza either, unless everybody in the whole joint is having some. And, while Texans don't shoot at the screen during westerns anymore, you'll be much happier if you know where to park. There is an almost universal pattern, diagrammed here:

Rows 10–15: Girls with girls, boys with boys, changing combinations. Snack bar area. Also loud and with high car-to-car traffic.

Rows 2–10: Families with large numbers of children. Close access to the playground. High noise area.

Front Row: People who are optically handicapped, who are wearing neck braces locked in an upright position, or who have taken mind-altering drugs and want to "get into" the picture.

HIPPIE REDNECKS

Texas is the birthplace of the Cosmic Cowboy. Hippies, or flower children, at least the California version, never existed in Texas outside of Austin. Those foolish enough to sympathize with the counterculture found that their lives became a series of bruises and DPS (Department of Public Safety)–initiated haircuts. As a result, the drug culture soon got hip to the fact that passing as a redneck provided the best disguise, and the forerunner of the Cosmic Cowboy was born. Soon enough, the druggies began to adopt the traditional values and work ethic of the classic Texas redneck. A last spasm of cultural osmosis created the final product, known lovingly as the Texas hippie redneck (THR). Hardworking and heavily drugged, THRs are easily identified. Most THRs work as tradesmen and bristle with tools of some sort. They drive pickups or vans, with four-wheel drive. Their vehicles are usually well maintained. Large dogs are a giveaway. Apparently, prolonged abuse of marijuana and beer produces an almost insurmountable desire to own a dog that weighs more than 85 pounds. Buck knives and chewing tobacco, plus a healthy respect for solar energy are other earmarks of the species. Outsiders dealing with THRs should realize that they embody both the best and the worst characteristics of two divergent cultures and act accordingly. No point in getting a chainsaw lobotomy as a result of a misdirected comment about Dolly Parton or Frank Zappa.

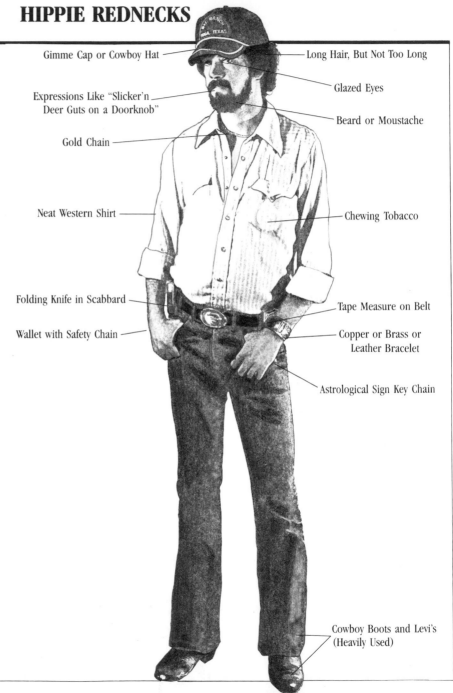

Gimme Cap or Cowboy Hat

Long Hair, But Not Too Long

Glazed Eyes

Expressions Like "Slicker'n Deer Guts on a Doorknob"

Beard or Moustache

Gold Chain

Neat Western Shirt

Chewing Tobacco

Folding Knife in Scabbard

Tape Measure on Belt

Wallet with Safety Chain

Copper or Brass or Leather Bracelet

Astrological Sign Key Chain

Cowboy Boots and Levi's (Heavily Used)

HUNTING

Texans have strong beliefs about the right to bear arms and to use them. The Texas heritage of range wars, rustlers, and assorted skirmishes has created a certain distinctive attitude toward hunting in Texas. Add to this the absolute rights of landowners in this state, and you can see that a casual hunting trip may turn out to be a semi-adventurous affair. This drawback has done nothing to discourage serious hunters, but it does make at least a rudimentary knowledge of traditions valuable if you intend to survive deer season.

Fences—Fences in Texas are more than demarcations of property. It's a good idea not to cross a fence unless you know whose land you're on. Irresponsible hunters have diminished not only the number of deer but also a great number of livestock, and ranchers find this less than humorous. Much less. In fact, it's not terribly hard to get shot for trespassing on some of the larger ranches if you're the argumentative sort.

Poodle Season—March 15 to May 15 in most major Texas cities, but worth a call to your local town hall for specific dates. Due to the toy's small size, no firearms are allowed. Usually baseball bats or clubs are used to bash these nasty little predators. The River Oaks Poodle Pound and Bazaar, held annually in Houston, attracts off-season sealers from all over the world.

Scopes—Useful for flatland varmint blasting but totally inappropriate for big-game hunting ranches. It's hard to tell what part of the animal you're aiming at when all you see is brown. Animals on the big-game ranches are trained to come for food at the honk of a jeep and ultimately the big sleep. A .45 automatic would seem more appropriate.

Dressing a Deer—The trick is getting their arms in the sleeves. Use some discretion; whitetails look terrible in plaids.

Squirrel Hunting—One of the few forms of wild-game hunting that can still be enjoyed in an urban environment, squirrel hunting is truly the sport of the masses. Each day, thousands of hunters turn out to stalk the asphalt byways in search of their wily prey. While an automobile is the only sporting weapon to use, many advanced hunters are beginning to switch to Mopeds for greater challenge and adventure.

Bow Hunters—Bow season opens two weeks before gun season for deer in Texas. That makes the season two weeks long. Anyone crazy enough to dress up in camouflage and creep around the woods during gun season should be heavily sedated and kept under close observation for a while.

FISHING

Texans approach fishing seriously. Very seriously. The state has a great number of game fish (both freshwater and saltwater), but one in particular is the popular choice above all others: the great Texas bass (GTB). Neither the largest nor the smallest of the bass family, the GTB is by far the most malicious, cunning creature ever to put fin to water. This accounts for the bitterness and respect that veteran fishermen feel toward the GTB and explains in part why, over the course of the last fifty years, every device known to man has been used to flush these shiny water weasels to the surface. For instance:

Calling All Fish—The old shockeroo, or "calling out for dinner" as it's euphemistically termed, is a favorite when 58 people show up for dinner. Take an old crank phone, put the wires in the water, and start cranking. Few people are aware that fish can dance, but you might be surprised what a little motivation like this can do. Of course, you'd better be sure you don't dial up a game warden or you might soon be dancing to a different tune. Avoid death by speargun by looking for divers before you try this one.

Lures, Flies, and Fishing Tackle—Largely regarded as useless against the GTB, these old-fashioned devices still represent the most common approach to trying to catch one. The success attributed to this hopelessly outdated equipment could be called misleading at best. The GTB is an easily bored creature, given to depression. Often the GTB will grow despondent and worry greatly over the spiraling cost of cole slaw. Frequently, he will hurl himself onto the nearest hook in the water rather than continue facing life with this issue in limbo. Thus, the great misconception begins, with the fisherman boasting of a catch that in reality is merely another ichthyosuicide.

Bass-a-boom-boom—Here's a fun one. Who knows how many fishermen would have given their right arm not to have tried this technique and ended up giving both (plus a lot of facial hair and the boat)? You just light a dynamite cap and toss it into the lake. Concussion city for anything in the water.

Helicopter—The expense of this effective technique makes it all but unknown to any save the wealthy. The hunter scans a lake for some shallow flats, lands quickly, and jumps out. Any corporate-sized whirlybird will be able to fan the water out before the fish catch on and try to leave. Just scoop the dullards up with nets or, better yet, have some minions grovel in the mud for you. Excellent sport and good eating.

STRANGE ON THE RANGE

You may encounter many unusual sights while roaming around Texas. Most are easily understood; others defy explanation. For example:

Small-Town Television News—Texas has more radio and television stations than any other state. A goodly number of would-be network anchormen start here and an almost equal number finish here. They are all to be found on small local newscasts. It's the home movies of public broadcasting—and quite enjoyable.

Boot Trays—You may notice someone dumping his cigarette ashes in his boots, especially if he's taken them off and is lying around a fire. While this practice may seem untidy, the ashes do absorb odor, and it beats flicking them on the floor and having to sweep them up later. A holdover from the days of stables, when a hot ash could start a fire and ranch hands didn't bathe very often.

Dr. Jekyll and Joe Bob Hyde—Urban professionals may undergo complete personality changes when they leave the city for a weekend in the country. In a misguided attempt to imitate cowboys, civilized, polite, educated, and well-mannered people will suddenly affect ignorant, coarse, and rude behavior. Cowboys would be among the first to take offense at these geeks.

Black Bottle—If you are traveling by car or truck and find a beer bottle propped up on the seat, half full of some unidentified foul black liquid, remember this: don't spill it on you or tip it over. You've located a local version of the portable spittoon. If you find this a disgusting thing to have around, take solace in the fact that occasionally its owner may take a swig from the wrong bottle while drinking beer.

BAD FACTS

Even Texans, friendly and loving as they are, are often irritated at the blunders of the outside world. And not without reason. For instance, not a single major network covers the Texas State Championship Domino Tournament, or the Kimble County Cow Kick, or any of the other biggies that happen all over our great state. But we're supposed to be enraptured watching ice hockey? Or relate to subways? That's ridiculous. And why do people think that *we're* supposed to pay for everything? We've helped a lot of foreigners get started. We sold Conrad Hilton his first hotel.

We'll sell boots to anyone. We have all those nasty offshore rigs that California and New Jersey didn't want cluttering up their coasts, but we share the oil. Few people think about it, but if Texans are supposed to be used to dealing with large amounts of money on a daily basis, then why has only one lonely Texan ever been Secretary of the U.S. Treasury? The federal government

wouldn't be in the mess it is now, that's for sure. Texas doesn't have a deficit budget. We'd shoot anybody crazy enough to suggest that move. Even an out-of-stater would think that at least one Texan would have been Secretary of Agriculture, but no, that would make too much sense. Texans are nothing if not forgiving, however. Many people probably think that Texans are just like everyone else, but now *you* know we're different. Maybe one day, with enough publicity, the rest of the country will change for the better—and then we'll all be Texans.